T0208602

Praying in the Shadows
Orihas in the Psalms

Iya A. C. Culver

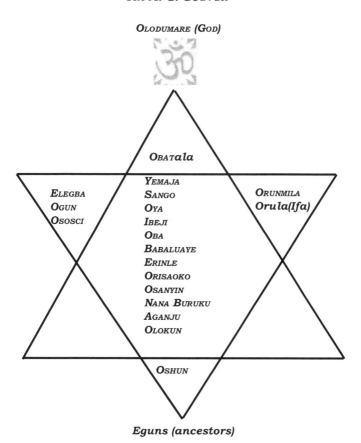

Olodumare (God)

Obatala

Elegba
Ogun
Ososci

Yemaja
Sango
Oya
Ibeji
Oba
Babaluaye
Erinle
Orisaoko
Osanyin
Nana Buruku
Aganju
Olokun

Orunmila
Orula(Ifa)

Oshun

Eguns (ancestors)

iUniverse, Inc.
New York   Bloomington

iUniverse books may be ordered through booksellers or by contacting:

iUniverse
1663 Liberty Drive
Bloomington, IN 47403
www.iuniverse.com
1-800-Authors (1-800-288-4677)

Because of the dynamic nature of the Internet, any Web addresses or links contained in this book may have changed since publication and may no longer be valid. The views expressed in this work are solely those of the author and do not necessarily reflect the views of the publisher, and the publisher hereby disclaims any responsibility for them.

ISBN: 978-1-4401-3979-6 (sc)
ISBN: 978-1-4401-3980-2 (ebook)

Printed in the United States of America

iUniverse rev. date: 04/20/2009

Praying in the Shadows

Orihas in the Psalms

Iya A. C. Culver

DTP: IFAGROUP.INFO

20094

PREFACE

A wise man who knows proverbs, reconciles difficulties.
Ashanti of Ghana

O come, let us sing unto the Lord: let us make a joyful noise to the rock of our salvation.
PS 95 V1

For thou, Lord art high above all the earth; thou art exalted far above all gods.
PS 97 V9

All traditional religions began in relationship to nature and communal, a human society. The love of the psalms in our journey comes from a synergy between the gospel songs of the Christians, Books of Wisdoms, and the African Traditional Religions – ATR.

A scattered people took up the banner of freedom and mercy that another did in another time. Sagely folks were on the ships who all ready understood the practical value of proverbs and the wisdom of elders and ancestors.

IFA was and is considered a book of wisdom in ATR and the Untied Nation's records of Antiquity. The Dilloggun with its cowrie's shells and Odu's were transported easier to the Caribbean's and finally came here to the States in full force after World War II. Why the divination system of IFA rules: it is still a narrative looking back at the great evolutions from West Africa to this hemisphere and into cyborg world

Iya, who was raised in traditional Spirituality, and has been an Orisa's Priest for over 18 years, was inspired to; give us a link between the Psalms and the Odu's. This effort has produced an interesting reference for all of us.

The references to a "rock" and "thou are exalted above all gods", shows clearer how our ancient poets described life, and that all religious traditions believe in a Sacred One. We all really sharing this ancient wisdom, separations are historical illusion. May we draw from this well and bring Long-life and Prosperity to our families and communities.

Nana Kwame "Osunwole" Toprah
Aka Kwame A.F. Copeland

INTRODUCTION

This book is about the hardship and hopes and dreams that Olodumare (god) the creator and all the Orishas gave to man. Orishas in all their aspects give regardless of the tribal, religion, or ancestry.

This book will touch hearts and souls of all who read it. Everyone has a spiritual up bringing, whether we accept it or not as we become adults. Once you walk through the waiting door the Path (journey) is laid out for you, yet we as humans have choices. In order to elevate one must study and learn the ways of the spirits, follow the rules and the calls, and even if we commit stupid acts;

Orishas offer learned lessons and possibilities. As I have told my children, godchildren, and clients. Orishas and Spirits do not like a smart-ass, being one risk the lost of spiritual protection and power for a long time, or ever again. Losing your spiritual protection from Eguns, Orisha, Angels, Third Eye (spirit eye), prayers go unheard and push come to worst - your life. The blessing is that you suffer the punishment and learn a lesson and can tell.

In Lucumi we have an odu (proverb) that says: What you don't learn in this life, you learn in the next. Is this one for you or what? How you like these apples?

The next part of this book is like making soup, good for the soul and warm to the bone.

My name is Iya Akosua Claudette Culver-Copeland. In 1988, I was crowned to Obatala and given the name Eni-Osun. It took me a while to understand my path. In 1989, just after making my year, my godfather Baba Shango-Dina passed in October. Since his Ile (Ocha House) was made Shango-Dina, by the way it means Shango's Fire. I kept the name and his Obatala pot was passed to me – by Oloduamare and Obatala himself. On till this day I do my best to keep his legacy and my own teaching and lessons alive..

This road hasn't been easy, but it has and still is a learning process, which will be my goal for the rest of my time on earth. I like to thank Baba Shango-Dina and my yubona, Baba Osungere   I thank them for loving me and allowing me to be free, faithful and resilient. They always have my back.

The goal of this book is how you can talk with the

Orishas, as shown to me; how to use and apply their names in the Psalms of the Old Testament and keep the purpose of the Psalm in tact. In using this method when called for it has worked. I have used it with clients and godchildren who focus on the purpose and the Orisha involved. Your prayer becomes more attuned to your situation

Prayer is something that is needed everyday. Not just because we want something from God and the Spirits; pray to show gratitude. Saying thank you goes a long way! To God and the Spirits, it does not matter where you were born. It is where you are going that counts. Like an Old Irish proverb: It is not what you came for, but what did you leave with. For an example, if your reading comes 7-7, Odi-Meji, you can read psalms 77 and asked and pray for guidance. This way, you will have a better understanding what has been said; the individual gains greater wisdom. Place your Spirit and Mind in order, for daily living, when following daily instructions, as given. Knowledge is given as a blessing or a curse, use it wisely

There is a proverb that states: Do be afraid to look at yourself
Meaning look at yourself without a physically mirror, let the world be your mirror. Make improvements, share your blessings and love, and you will be blessed in returned.

In the confused world that we are living in today, people are all in hurry and for what? It's just a world full of chaos and misunderstandings. Why! Because life means nothing to most people, today; it's just the Love of money in their pockets, living in a time were no one really cares about a human being. In today's world, if you find someone who really cares or even take the time to help you, or hurt your feelings to help you, hold on to the person with all might, and heart. Our so-called feeling brings on the problems and hardship and the heartache, humans love to carried and hold on to. Now it is the time to go back to basic! Hand clapping, and old sayings of the grandmothers and big mamma's of yesterday.

This is also a time to honor the grandpas and daddies who cared about the family structures. If history has taught us anything is to remember the elders, because their wisdoms are diamond in a rough - beauty to always be passed on. These Psalms are the diamonds they passed on to us. And just like a diamond, it can be shaped different and presented differently, yet it is still a diamond.

Today I will try to teach you, what Olodumare and Spirits has shown and taught me. So far, it has been very successful! Let me warn you have a good and kind heart, and sound mind, because God, Spirits, Orishas, and you ancestors or Egun don't play. Always try to be of good character and truthful in prays, and your requests in time they will answer and show you the way.

Growing up in a Spiritual Christian, I learn to pray at a very early age. I began my spiritual journey at the age of 16. Now that I have reached my 50th's, I am still growing and I covered all types of learning grounds. I, too, have gone through my ups and downs, win and losses, and still kept faith in Olodumare, Orishas,

Ancestors, Egungun, Angels, and Saints of the Church - a long with any other paths of these forces that came together.

I also met spirituals person along the way, many are gone now, and met many new ones. Never to young or old, to listen, to learn, and to sit! Remember old saying: Prayer changes things!

MAY

Olodumare
My father Obatala
My mother Yemoja
My mother Kali
My father Shiva
My protector Hanuman
Place your heart, your Ori (head) and Spirit in the right Path! Ashe

DEDICATION

To my Eguns: Mojuba
My mother – Rev. Jimmie Lee Johnson Culver-Mooring – 1988
My father – Mr. Willie Lang Culver – 1996
My "step-father" – Mr. James Henry Mooring – 1977
My grandparents – Mr. & Mrs. Jim Johnson Jr.
My grandparents – Mr. & Mrs. Robert Culver Sr.
My Ocha Family
My Ocha Grandmother – Iya Mercedes "Oban Yoko" Nobles – 1989
My Godfather Baba Jose Miguel "Sango Dina" Alicica Jr. - 1989
Iya Asunta Serrano – 1988
Iya Bettey "Sangofunke" Barney – 1988
Iya (Mama) Keke "Oshunfunke" Boyce – 1996

To a special friend and Sister in Love
Iya (Nana) Aba Nson Osunyomi – 1996

To Living:
My Sons; Kwabena Leonard J. Culver; Kwesi Joseph E.
Culver; My Ajubonia Baba Lazzaro "Osungere"
To the elders and godchildren of Ile Sango Dina of
Brooklyn NY
To all the folks close to us I love you all and a special
thank you to my very best friend/partner who walked
me through this project and cheered me on and did the
typing and DTP. With all my love – Nana Kwame
Baakan "Osunwole" Toprah aka Kwame A. F. Copeland

There are hundreds and thousands of books written on
the Orishas and many versions of The Book of Psalms. I
choice two I enjoy and utilize in my practice. With each
psalm there will be a corresponding odu giving an
understanding to proverbs. There are 150 psalms and I
will provide, also corresponding color of candles and oil
for each. Now let's start the process of learning how to
work and build a new you!
For starters here the list of all Orishas and their numbers
and themes from 1611 KJV's Psalms to understand
where I'm coming from and going to:

Elegba	1, 3, 21, 101
Ogun	3, 4, 7
Osocsi	3, 7

Oya	9
Shango/ Sango	4, 6
Osun/ Oshun	5
Olokun	7
Babalu- Aiye	13, 17
Aganju	6, 9
Ibeji/ Ibeyi	2
Obatala	8
Oba	9
Osanyin	3
Erinle	7
Egun	9
Nana Buruku	13, 17

Orisa Oko	2
Orunmila /Orunla	16
Yemoja/ Yemaya	7

The Odu's will be taken from: **THE DILLOGGUN** (1)

THE SPIRITUAL & PHYSICAL FOUNDATIONS OF THE ORISHA

ELEBGA: Opens the doors and to make our Paths smoother. So that our prayers and offerings are accepted by God (Olodumare) and Orishas and Ancestors (Eguns) and also helps in critical dealings of Justice, Health, Jobs, Home, Family, excreta.

OGUN - Clear a Way with his wisdom and tools for life existence and Health, Jobs, Court Case, Cars, All metal substances.

OSOSCI - Brings Justice within and out of Spiritual and Physical Law; Knowledge of herbs and Magic; hits the target; Spiritual Karma; physically plain; and places order in Divine Order

OYA - Brings changes in Mental, Spiritual, Physical, Growth, Health, jobs, Family, Home, Land. Since she owns the wind and rain, she pushes away what not needed and brings what is needed

SHANGO - Brings Courage, Strength, Wisdom, Cleans by Fire, Prayers. He makes you look more at yourself or the problems and situation that you face in your daily life. Helps bring money when needed works with Oshun on that.

OSHUN - Brings forth Love of Self, Family, Community, Music, Art, Heal the Blood, All women problems, Deals with children in kindness. Help brings forth money as needed not as desired.

OLOKUN - Bring you closer to your ancestors and gives you stability in your life. He also clears up all negative karma in your family line.

BABALU **A**IYE - Deals with all illness that plagues the world. Comforter with a listening ear and shoulder to cry on when you feel like no one in the world understands you or don't care; He'll be your crutch; He'll lift you up.

AGANJU - Helps with health problems and carry you over obstacles in your mind, spirit, body and fights for justice as needed.

IBEJI - The children, they bring Love, Joy, Happiness, Money into our lives and hold families together. They help in marriage problems, also.

OBATALA - Brings the Head (Ori) to the highest level of conscience as possibility. He brings clarity in thinking, calmness, and coolness. He works with the inner spirit - Elder, which is located mole of the head. He works, also with the third eye, located and eyebrows and forehead.

OBA - She brings stability in homes and marriages. Helps to bring together wife and husband, creating faithfulness between then. Builds home into a stronger foundation.

OSANYIN- Helps with God (Olodumare) and nature to bring forth food and herbs for mankind and all the animals.

ERINLE - Brings Knowledge of medicine to spiritual healers and all physician medical field including Nurses, excreta.

EGUN - Ancestors who guides us in the spirit world through prays and offerings.

NANA BURUKU - Works close with Babalu Aiye, bringing balance to illness and health.

ORISHA OKO - He brings forth the food for mankind and animals; he heals the earth himself.

ORUNMILA - Deals with Density of the individuals and the cosmic sense of the word. He guides the person who is either searching for truth or in a bad state of confusion. He settles the misunderstanding of one-self and among the Orishas, with the permission from God - for human needs.

YEMOJA - Mother of the Earth and of the Heavens. She helps bring forth children, and with nourishing nature: she also assists with all aspects of learning. She, also, raises all the children of the Orishas and the World.

UNDERSTANDING THE FUNDAMENTALS USAGE OF THE PSALMS.

My mother, the late Rev. J. Culver-Mooring taught this method not only in our home when she taught spirituality classes but in the church St. Michael Spiritualist Church – Brooklyn NY 1968.
This is the method and system she taught:
1) Kabalistic Conceptual Of Psalms
2) Modern Theological Concepts of the Psalm
3) Synthesis of the Psalms
4) Met ha physical Purpose of the Psalms
5) Southern belief and traditional usage of Psalms with - herbs, oils, candles, incense, baths, flora washes.
6) Mediation Purpose of Psalms
7) Believe in the assistance of Angles, Orishas, Spirit-guides, Saints of different faith or religious background.

PSALM 46
Title - God is our refuge and strength, yet this psalm with PS 45 title: A song for the King's Marriage, is used to help heal and bring peace between a wife and a husband. These Psalms along can also be used in helping with Luck, Job, Money, Home Life, Court Case, Children, excreta. So don't let the Title of the Psalms

confuse you. Some of these methods are used in this field of knowledge - within spiritual work. The point is all this different methods are used to help the person - spiritual, mentally, physically, and financially

THEMES FROM THE PSALMS (2)

Psalm 1 – The Righteous and the Ungodly

Psalm 2 – The Reign of the Lord's Anointed

Psalm 3 – A Morning Prayer of Trust in God

Psalm 4 – An Evening Prayer of Trust in God

Psalm 5 – A Prayer for Protection

Psalm 6 - A Prayer for Mercy in Time of Trouble

Psalm 7 – Prayer for Vindication

Psalm 8 – God's Glory and Man's Honor

Psalm 9 – Thanksgiving for God's Justice

Psalm 10 – A Prayer for the Overthrow of the Wicked

Psalm 11 – The Refuge of the Upright

Psalm 12 – A Prayer for Help against the Wicked

Psalm 13 – A Prayer for Help in Trouble

Psalm 14 - The Folly and Wickedness of Men

Psalm 15 – The Inhabitants of God's Holy Hill

Psalm 16 – A Good Heritage

Psalm 17 – A Prayer for Protection against Oppressors

Psalm 18 – Thanksgiving for Deliverance

Psalm 19 – The Works and Word of God

Psalm 20 – A Prayer for Victory

Psalm 21 – Praise for Deliverance from the Enemy

Psalm 22 – A Cry of Anguish and Song of Praise

Psalm 23 – The Lord Is My Shepherd

Psalm 24 – The King of Glory

Psalm 25 – A Prayer for Guidance, Pardon and
Protection

Ethical Themes

PS 1 – Baba Eshu Elegba:

Verse 1 – Blessed is the man that walked not in the
    council of the ungodly nor standeth in
    the in the way of sinners, nor sitten in the seat of
    the scornful.

Verse 5 – Therefore the ungodly shall not stand in the
    judgment nor sinners in the
    congregation of the righteous.

Odu – Just as goodness gives birth to goodness so shall
    evil always conceive evil.

Lights – White Candle w Clearance oil

PS 2 – Baba Obatala:

Verse 1 – Why do the heathen rage and the people
    imagine a vain thing?

Verse 4 – He that sitten in the Heavens shall laugh: the
    Lord shall have them in derision.

Odu – Where there are arguments there can be no peace!

Lights – White Candle w Peace oil

PS 3 – Baba Ogun:

Verse 1 – Lord how are they increased that troubles me!
    Many are they that rise up against me.

Verse 3 – But thou O' Lord are a shield for me; my glory
    and the lifter up of mine head.

Odu – As you have sown so shall you reap.

Lights – Green Candle w High John oil

PS 4 – BABA SANGO/SHANGO:

Verse 1 – Hear me when I call, O God of my righteous
ness! Thou hast enlarged me when
  I was in distress; have mercy upon me, and hear
  my prayer.

Verse 5 – Offer the sacrifices of righteousness, and out
  your trust in the Lord.

Odu – Unseen things are best left unseen

Lights – White or Red Candle w Fruit of Life oil

PS 5 – IYA OSHUN/OSUN:

Verse 1 – Give ear to my words, O Lord; consider my
  meditation.

Verse 11 – But let all those that put trust in thee rejoice;
  let them ever shout for joy, because thou defendest
  them; let them also that love thy name be joyful in
  thee.

Odu – While your tongue is your luck it is also your
  digrace.

Lights – Yellow Candle w Shut Up oil

PS 6 – BABA SANGO/SHANGO:

Verse 1 – O Lord rebuke me not in thine anger, neither
  chasten me in thy hot displeasure.

Verse 3 – Return, O Lord, deliver my soul: Oh save me
  for thy mercies' sake.

Odu – While all humans are born sincere all will die
  liars.

Lights – White Candle w Sandalwood oil

PS 7 – Iya Yemeja/Yemanja:

Verse 1 – O Lord my God in thee do I put my trust: Save me from all them that persecute me, and deliver me.

Verse 15 – He made a pit, and digged it, and is fallen into the ditch which he made.

Odu – This is where the hole (grave) was first dug.

Lights – Blue or White Candle w Peace oil

PS 8 – Baba Obatala:

Verse 1 – O Lord, Our Lord, how excellent is thy name in all the earth! Who hast set thy glory above the heavens.

Verse 9 – O Lord, Our Lord, how excellent is thy name in all the earth!

Odu – Love yourself for only then can you love others.

Lights – White Candle w Lily of the Valley oil

PS 9 – Iya Oya Yansa:

Verse 1 – I will praise thee, O Lord, with my whole heart; I will show forth all thy marvelous works.

Verse 9 – The Lord also will be a refuge for the oppresses, a refuge in times of trouble.

Odu – You can be your worst enemy.

Lights – Brown Candle w Meditation oil

PS 10 – Baba Eshu Elegba:

Verse 1 – Why standest thou afar off, O Lord? Why hidest thou, thyself in times of trouble?

Verse 12 – Arise, O Lord: O God, lift up thine hand: For

get not the humble.

Odu – Where the curse was born.

Lights – Red & Blue Candle w Reversible oil

PS 11 – BABA BABALU AYE:

Verse 1 – In the Lord I put my trust: Hasten ye to my
soul, flee as a bird to your mountain?

Verse 3 – If the foundation be destroyed, what can the
righteous do?

Odu – The hurt that one causes others is the hurt that
they will cause him.

Lights – Purple Candle w Special Favor oil.

PS 12 – BABA SANGO/SHANGO:

Verse 1 – Help, Lord for the godly man easeth; for the
faithful fail from among the children of men.

Verse 3 - The Lord shall cut off all flattening lips, and the
tongue that speaketh proud things.

Odu – When rough waters come, even a ship will sink.

Lights – Red Candle w Protection oil

PS 13 – IYA NANA BURUKU:

Verse 1 – How long will thou forget me, O Lord? For
ever? How long will thou hide thy face from me?

Verse 6 – I will sing unto the Lord, because he hath dealt
bountifully with me.

Odu – Only strength can destroy evil.

Lights – Purple Candle w Hyssop oil

PS 14 – IYA OSHUN/OSUN:

Verse 1 – The fool haith said in his heart, there is no
God. They are corrupt, they have done
abominable works there is none that doeth good.

Verse 5 – There were they in great fear: For God is in the
generation of the righteous

Odu – Lies bring arguments.

Lights – Yellow Candle w Orange Blossom oil

PS 15 – BABA SANGO/SHANGO:

Verse 1 – Lord, who shall abide in the tabernacle? Who
shall dwell in the Holy Hill?

Verse 5 – He that putteth not out his money to usury,
nor taketh reward against the innocent, he that
doeth these thinks shall never be moved.

Odu – Strong people work to make others strong.

Lights – White Candle w Cassia oil

PS 16 – BABA ORUNMILA:

Verse 1 – Pleasure me, O God: For in thee do I put my
trust.

Verse 7 – I will bless the Lord, who has given me
counsel: my reins also instruct me in the night
seasons.

Odu – A single holy word does make good than a load
of profane speeches.

Lights – Green & Yellow Candle w Holy oil

PS 17 – BABA BABALU AIYE:

Verse 1 – Hear the right, O Lord, attend unto my cry;
give ear unto my prayer, that goeth not out of

feigned lips.

Verse 8 – Keep me as the apple of the eye; hide me under the shadow of the wings.

Odu – Kneeling, one talks with God.

Lights – White Candle w Keep Away Enemies oil

PS 18 – BABA AGANJU:

Verse 1 – I will love thee, O Lord, my strength.

Verse 3 – I will call upon the Lord, who is worthy to be praised; so shall I be saved from mine enemies.

Odu – Rain water is God's water wash your self in it.

Lights – Brown Candle w Helping Hands oil

PS 19 – IYA OSHUN/OSUN:

Verse 1 – The Heavens declare the glory of God; and the firmament showed his handiwork.

Verse 8 – The statues of the Lord are right, rejoicing the Heart: The commandment of the Lord is pure, enlightening the eyes.

Odu – A bell that has no clapper cannot call anyone's attention.

Lights – Orange Candle w Honey oil

PS 20 – IBEYI/IBEJI:

Verse 1 – The Lord hear thee in the day of trouble; the name of the God of Jacob defend thee.

Verse 4 – Grant thee according to thine own heart, and fulfill all thy counsel.

Odu – One does not know today what will be done tomorrow.

Lights – Blue & Red Candle w Coconut oil

PS 21 – BABA ESHU ELEGBA:

Verse 1 – The King shall joy in thy strengthen, O Lord;
and in thy salvation how greatly shall he rejoice!

Verse 13 – Be thou exalted, Lord, in thine own strength:
So will we sing and praise thy power.

Odu – They want to destroy the king by killing him with
arrow.

Lights – Red & Black Candle w Just Judge oil

PS 22 – BABA OGUN:

Verse 1 – My God, My God, why hast, thou forsaken
me? Why are thou so far from helping me, and
from the words of roaring?.

Verse 5 – They cries unto thee, and were delivered: They
trusted in thee, and were not confounded.

Odu – No one knows what lies at the bottom of the
ocean.

Lights – Green Candle w Peaceful Home oil

PS 23 – IYA OSHUN/OSUN:

Verse 1 – The Lord is my shepherd; I shall not want.

Verse 6 – Surely goodness and merry shall follow me all
the days of my life: And I will dwell in the House
of the Lord forever.

Odu – Just as there are rivers in the earth, so are there
rivers in the veins.

Lights – Green Candle w Money oil

PS 24 – BABA OBATULA:

Verse 1 – The earth is the Lord's and the fullness there of; the world, and they that dwell therein.

Verse 5 – He shall receive the blessings from the Lord, and righteousness from the God of his salvation.

Odu – The head first created will, not fail to prosper in the market.

Lights – White Candle w Almond oil

PS 25 – BABA OSOSCI/OCHOCI:

Verse 1 – Unto Thee, O Lord, Do I lift up my soul!

Verse 7 – Remember not the sins of my youth, nor my transgression: Awarding to thy mercy remember thou thy goodness' sake, O Lord.

Odu – Don't leave your customs.

Lights – Blue or Purple Candle w Frankincense oil

PS 26 – BABA OBATALA:

Verse 1 – Judge me, O Lord; for I have walked in mine integrity: I have trusted also in the Lord; there fore; I shall not slide.

Verses 12 – My foot standeth in an even place: in the congregation will I bless the Lord.

Odu – Where there is life there is always hope.

Lights – White Candle w Kindly Spirit oil

PS 27 – IYA OYA YANSA:

Verse 1 – The Lord is my light, and my salvation; whom shall I fear? The Lord is the strengthen of my life; of whom shall I be afraid?.

Verses 7 – Hear, O Lord, when I cry with my voice:

Have mercy also upon me, and answer me.

Odu – Humility will win the battle.

Lights – Brown Candle w Camphor oil

PS 28 – BABA OBATALA:

Verse 1 – Unto thee will I Cry; O Lord my rock; be not
silent to me: lest, if this be silent to me, I become
like them that go down into the pit.

Verses 6 – Blessed be the Lord, because he hath heard
the voice of my supplication.

Odu – Forgive those who curse you for he who forgive is
saved.

Lights – White Candle w Envy oil

PS 29 – BABA ORISHO OKO:

Verse 1 – Give unto the Lord, O ye mighty, give unto the
Lord glory and strength.

Verses 9 – The voice of the Lord maketh the hinds to
calve, and discovereth the forests: and in His
Temple doeth every one speak of His Glory.

Odu – Why take on the troubles of others when one has
problems of one's own.

Lights – White Candle w Miracle oil

PS 30 – BABA ESHU ELEGBA:

Verse 1 – I will extol thee, O Lord; for thou hast lifted me
up, and hast not made my foes to rejoice over me.

Verses 10 – Hear, O Lord and have mercy upon me:
Lord, be thou my helper.

Odu – Turn tears into laughter.

Lights – White Candle w Ode to Joy oil

PS 31 – Baba Sango/Shango:

Verse 1 – In thee O Lord, do I put my trust; let me never be ashamed: deliver me into righteousness.

Verses 9 – Have mercy upon me, O Lord, for I am in trouble: mine eye is consumed with grief, yes, and my soul and my belly.

Odu – If you put ones heart into one's work all things will come out well..

Lights – Red Candle w All Spice oil

PS 32 – Iya Oshun/Osun:

Verse 1 – Blessed is he whose transgression is forgiven, whose sin is covered.

Verses 7 – Thou are my hiding place; thou hast preserving me from trouble; thou shall compass me about with songs of deliverance. Selah.

Odu – Life is beautiful do not destroy your own beauty.

Lights – Yellow Candle w Altar of Rose oil

PS 33 – Baba Sango/Shango:

Verse 1 – Rejoice in the Lord, O Ye righteous: for praise is comely for the upright.

Verses 6 – By the word of the Lord were the heavens made; and all the hast of wisdom by the bread of his mouth.

Odu – Quietly I shall go and quietly I shall come.

Lights – Red Candle w Crown of Success oil

PS 34 – BABA OSOSCI/OSHOSI:

Verse 1 – I will bless the Lord at all times: His praises shall continually be in my mouth.

Verses 15 – The eyes of the Lord are upon the righteous, and His ears are open unto their cry.

Odu – Those who laugh at you today will beg you tomorrow.

Lights – Purple Candle w Fiery Walk of Protection oil

PS 35 – BABA OBATALA:

Verse 1 – Plead my cause, O Lord, with thou that strive with me: fight against those that fight against me.

Verses 3 – Draw out also the spear, and stop the way against them that persecute me: Say unto my soul, I am thy salvation.

Odu – The dove was once menaced by the snails, so he opened his wings and flew away.

Lights – White Candle w Dove Blood oil

PS 36 – IYA OYA YANSA:

Verse 1– Transgressing of the wicked saith within my heart, that there is no fear of God before his eyes.

Verse 9 – For with thee is the fountain of Life: in thy Light shall we see Light.

Odu – Stay to yourself

Lights - Brown Candle w Attar of Jasmine Oil.

PS 37 – BABA ESHU ELEGBA:

Verse 1 – Fret not thyself because of evil doers neither be envious against the workers of iniquity.

Verse 13 – The Lord shall laugh at him: For he seeth that

his day is coming.

Odu – Wherever you turn, there are traps and prisons

Lights – Red/Black Candle w Jinix Removing oil

PS 38 – BABA BABALUAIYE:

Verse 1 – O Lord, rebuke me not in the wrath neither chasten me in the hot displeasure.

Verse 6 – I am troubled. I am been down greatly; I go mourning all the day long.

Odu – While the vulture is hungry, catastrophe will feed him.

Lights – Black Candle w Uncrossing oil

PS 39 – BABA SANGO/SHANGO:

Verse 1 – I said I will take heed to my ways, that I sin not with my tongue: I will keep my mouth with a bridle, while the wicked is before me.

Verse 7 – And now Lord, what wait I for? My hope is in thee.

Odu – Flies cannot enter a closed mouth.

Lights - Red Candle w Spikenard oil

PS 40 – BABA SANGO/SHANGO:

Verse 1– I waited patiently for the Lord; and he inclined unto me, and heard my cry.

Verse 8 – I delight to do thy will, O my God: Yea thy law is within my heart.

Odu – Look forward and look backward

Lights – White Candle w Benzoin oil

PS 41 – IYA OSHUN/OSUN:

Verse 1– Blessed is he that considerate the poor: the Lord will deliver him in time of trouble.

Verse 12 – And as for me thou upholds me in mine integrity, and settiest me before thy face forever.

Odu – He who forgiving is saved, he who does not is doomed.

Lights – Yellow Candle w Orris Root oil

PS 42 – BABA SANGO/SHANGO:

Verse 1– As the heart panteth after the water brooks, so panteth my soul a thee after thee, O God.

Verse 6 – O my God, my soul is cast down within me: therefore will I remember thee from the Lamb of Jordon, and of this Her'monies from the Hik Mizar

Odu – There is a rocky path before you.

Lights – Red Candle w Bay oil

PS 43 – BABA OSOSCI/OSHOSCI:

Verse 1– Judge me, O God and plead my cause against an ungodly nation: O deliver me from the deceitful an unjust man

Verse 4 – Then I will go unto the alter of God, unto God my exceeding joy: Yea upon the harp will I praise thee, O God, My God.

Odu – A single man can save his people.

Lights – Blue Candle w Anise oil

PS 44 – BABA OBATALA:

Verse 1– We have heard with our ears, O God, our

fathers have told us, what work thou didst in their days, the time of old.

Verse 8 – In God we boast, all day long, and praise thy name forever. Selah

Odu – All the fingers are children of the same hand, and none can separate.

Lights – White Candle w Heliotrope oil

PS 45 – Iya Oya Yansa:

Verse 1– My Heart is inditing a good matter: I speak of the things which I have made touching the King: My tongue is the pen of a ready writer

Verse 17 – I will make thy name to be remembered in all generation: Therefore shall the people praise thee for someone to talk

Odu – Death is taking a stroll, looking for someone to take.

Lights – Brown Candle w Satan Be Gone oil

PS 46– Baba Babaolaiye:

Verse 1– God is our refuge and strengthen a very present held in trouble.

Verse 8 – Come, Behold the works of the Lord, what desolations he hath made in the Earth.

Odu – The explosion of the volcano is your daily life.

Lights – White Candle w St Lazarus oil

PS 47 – Iya Yemoja/Yemanja:

Verse 1– O clap your hands, all we people; shout unto God with the voice of triumph.

Verse 3 – He shall choose our inheritance for us, the

Excellency of Jacob whom he lived. Selah

Odu – All that glitters is not gold.

Lights – Blue Candle w Lotus oil

PS 48 – BABA ESHU ELEGBA:

Verse 1– Great is the Lord, and greatly to be praised in
the City of our God, in the mountain of His
Holiness.

Verse 14 – For this God is our God forever and ever: He
will be our guide even into Death.

Odu – A king dies, and a king is born.

Lights – White Candle w All Saints oil

PS 49 – BABA OBATALA:

Verse 1– Hear this, all ye people; gives ears, all ye
inhabitants of the world.

Verse 19 – He shall go the generation of his fathers: They
shall never see light.

Odu – [There will be] Treason among friends.

Lights – White Candle w Olive oil

PS 50 – IYA OSHUN/OSUN:

Verse 1– The Mighty God, even the Lord, hath spoken,
and called the Earth,from the rising of the sun
unto the going down there of.

Verse 5 – gather my Saints together unto me; those that
have made a covenant with me, by sacrifice.

Odu – There is a proper time for everything.

Lights – Yellow Candle w Shi Shi oil

PS 51 – Baba Obatala:

Verse 1– Have mercy upon me, O God, according to thy loving-kindness: according unto the multitude of thy tender mercies blot out my transgressions.

Verse 4 – Against thee, thee only, have I sinned and done this evil in thy sight: that thou mightiest be justified when thou speakest, and be clear when thou judgest.

Odu – Jealousy is the mother of mistrust.

Lights – White Candle w Protection from Envy oil

PS 52 – Iya Yemeja/Yemanja:

Verse 1– Why boastest thou thyself in mischief, O Mighty Man? The goodness of God endureth continually

Verse 8 – But I am like a green olive tree in the House of God: I trust in the mercy of God forever and ever

Odu – Do not abandon certainties for the unknown.

Lights – Blue Candle w Balsam oil.

PS 53 – Iya Oshun/Osun:

Verse 1– The fool hath said in his heart, there is no God. Corrupt are they, and have done abominable iniquity: there is none that dueth good.

Verse 3 – Every one of them is gone back: they are altogether become filthy; there is none that doeth good, no, not one.

Odu – Your enemy will do you evil, and yet he will do you good.

Lights – Yellow Candle w Cast Off Evil oil.

PS 54 – IYA OSHUN/OSUN:

Verse 1– Save me, O God, by thy name, and judge me by thy strength.

Verses 3 – For strangers are risen up against me, and oppressors seek after my soul: they have set God before them. Selah

Odu – If the rain does not fall, the corn does not grow.

Lights – Yellow Candle w Mango oil

PS 55 – IYA OSHUN/OSUN:

Verse 1– Give ear to my prayer, O God; and hide not thyself from my supplication.

Verse 14 – We talk sweet counsel together, and walked unto the House of God in company.

Odu – Promises made must be kept.

Lights – Yellow Candle w Vanilla oil

PS 56 – IYA OSHUN/OSUN:

Verse 1– Be merciful unto me, O God: for man swallow me up, he fighting daily oppresseth me.

Verse 10 – In God will I praise His word: In the Lord will I praise His word.

Odu – The bitterness of the world is carried with you.

Lights – Yellow Candle w Vencedor oil.

PS 57 – BABA ORUNMILA:

Verse 1– Be merciful unto me, o God be merciful unto me: for my soul trusteth in thee: yea, in the shadow of thy wings will I make my refuge, until these calamities be overpast.

Verse 10 – For thy mercy is great unto the heavens, and

thy truth unto the clouds.

Odu – Prepare for war.

Lights – Green & Yellow Candle w Verbena oil

PS 58 – IYA OSHUN/OSUN:

Verse 1– Do ye indeed speak righteousness, o congregation? Do ye judge uprightly, O Ye Sons of Men?

Verse 10 – The righteous shall rejoice when He seeth the vengeance: He shall wash his feet in the blood of the wicked.

Odu – Do not cry in misery; it will only make things worst.

Lights – Yellow Candle w Red Rose oil

PS 59 – IYA OSHUN/OSUN:

Verse 1– Deliver me from mine enemies, O my God: defend me from them that rise up against me.

Verse 16 – But I willing of the paser, yea I will sing aloud of the mercy in the morning: for thou hast been my defense and refuge in the day of my trouble.

Odu – Calmness and coolness save from destruction.

Lights – Yellow Candle w Sweet Pea oil

PS 60 – BABA SANGO/SHANGO:

Verse 1– O God, thou hast cast us off, thou hast scattered us, thou hast been displeased; O turn thyself to us again.

Verse 4 – Thou hast given a banner to them that fear thee, that it may be displayed because of the truth. Selah

Odu – A patient man can become the king of the world.

Lights – Red Candle w St. Barbara oil

PS 61 – Baba Sango/Shango:

Verse 1– Hear my cry, O God; attend unto prayer.

Verse 6 – Thou will prolong the King's life: and His
years as many generations.

Odu – Be frank and speak your heart.

Lights – White Candle w Lime oil

PS 62 – Baba Obatala:

Verse 1– Truly my soul waiteth upon God: from Him
cometh my salvation.

Verse 4 – They only consult to cast Him down from His
Excellency: they delight in lies: they bless with
their mouth, but they curse inwardly. Selah.

Odu – One can be fooled by looks and appearances

Lights – White Candle w Orchid oil

PS 63 – Baba Ogun:

Verse 1– O God, thou art my God, early will I see thee:
my soul thirsteth for thee, my flesh longeth for
thee in a day and thisty land, where no water

Verse 11 – But the King shall rejoice in God; even one
that swearth by Him shall Glory: but the mouth of
them that speak lies shall be stopped.

Odu – You work hard, and yet your work is always bad.

Lights – Green Candle w Steady Work oil

PS 64 – Baba Obatala:

Verse 1– Hear my voice, O God, in my prayer: preserve my life from fear of the enemy.

Verse 10 – The righteous shall be glad in the Lord, and shall trust in Him; and all the upright in heart shall Glory.

Odu – Always give respect to the Orishas.

Lights – White Candle w Rose (white) oil

PS 65 – Baba Orunmila:

Verse 1– Praise waiteth for thee, O God, in Zion: and unto thee shall the vow be preformed.

Verse 10 – Thou waterest the ridges there of abundantly: Thou settles the furrows thereof: Thou makest it soft with showers: Thou blessest the springing thereof.

Odu – If the heart is clean, it holds more value than money.

Lights – Green & Yellow Candle w Acacia oil

PS 66 – Baba Sango/Shango:

Verse 1– Make a joyful noise unto God, all ye lands.

Verse 4 – All the earth shall worship thee, and shall sing unto thee; they shall sing to thy name. Selah

Odu – He who doesn't knows dies, while he who does know lives.

Lights – Red Candle w Banana oil

PS 67 – Baba Sango/Shango:

Verse 1– God be merciful unto us, and bless us; and cause His face to shine upon us; Selah

Verse 5 – Let the people praise thee, O God; let all the
people praise thee.

Odu – While a dog has four legs, it still walks only one
path.

Lights – White Candle w Carnation oil

PS 68 – BABA OBATALA:

Verse 1– Let God arise, let enemies be scattered: let them
also that hate Him flee before Him.

Verse 4 – Sing unto God, sing praises to His name: extol
Him that rideth upon the Heavens by His name
Jah, and rejoice before Him.

Odu – The ears cannot top the head; therefore, respect
the elders.

Lights – White Candle w Rose Geranium oil

PS 69 – EGUNS:

Verse 1– Save me, O God; for the waters are come in
unto my soul.

Verse 14 – Deliver me out of the mire, and let me not
sink: let me delivered from them that hate, and out
of deep water.

Odu – When you run, run with prudence.

Lights – White Candle w Spirit oil

PS 70 – IYA YEMOJA/YEMANJA:

Verse 1– Make haste, O God, to deceiver me; make haste
to help me. O Lord

Verse 5 – But I am poor and needy; make haste unto me,
O God: thou art my help and my deliver; O Lord,
make no tarrying.

Odu – The biggest fish will be caught in the biggest
ocean with the best bait and a little luck.

Lights – Blue Candle w Angelica oil

PS 71 – Iya Yemoja/Yemanja:

Verse 1– In thee O Lord, do I put my trust: let me never
be put to confusion.

Verse 14 – But I will hope continually, and will yet
praise thee more and more.

Odu – The rich will envy the poor.

Lights – Blue Candle w Hawthorn oil

PS 72 – Baba Obatala:

Verse 1– Give the King thy judgments, O God, and thy
righteousness unto the King's son.

Verse 13 – He shall spare the poor and needy, and shall
save the souls of the needy.

Odu – Riches will come when the business is born.

Lights – White Candle w Wealthy Way oil

PS 73 – Baba Ogun:

Verse 1– Truly God is good to Israel, even to such as are
of a clean heart.

Verse 26 – My flesh and my heart failed: but God is the
strength of my heart, and my portion forever.

Odu – Look at what is in front of your eyes.

Lights – Green Candle w Dragon's Blood oil

PS 74 – Baba Olokun:

Verse 1 – O God, why hast cast us off forever? Why doth

thou anger smoke against the sheep of thy
pasture?

Verse 20 – Have respect unto the covenant: for he dark
places of the earth are full of the habitations of
cruelty.

Odu – No one knows what lies at the bottom of the
ocean.

Lights – Gray Candle w Thyme oil

PS 75 – IYA YEMOJA/YEMANJA:

Verse 1– Unto thee, O God, do we give thanks, unto thee
do we give thanks: for that thy name is near thy
wondrous works declare.

Verse 7 – But God is the judge: He putteth down one,
and setteth up another.

Odu – All things are good to eat, but not all thinks are
good to say.

Lights – Blue Candle w Mugwort oil

PS 76 – BABA SANGO/SHANGO:

Verse 1– In Judah is God known; His name is Grace in
Israel.

Verse 11 – Vow, and pay unto the Lord your God: let all
that be round about Him bring presents unto Him
that ought to be feared.

Odu – Do not follow your bad impulses; go only with
those that are good.

Lights – Red Candle w Vision oil

PS 77 – IYA YEMOJA/YEMANJA:

Verse 1– I cried unto God with my voices, even unto

God with my voices, even unto God with my
voice; and He gave ear unto me.

Verse 19 – Thy way is in the sea, and thy path in this
great water, and thy footsteps are not known

Odu – Everyone makes sure that he does his things with
care so they come out well.

Lights – Blue Candle w Sea Queen oil

PS 78 – BABA OGUN:

Verse 1 – Give ear, O my people, to my law; incline your
ears to the words of my mouth.

Verse 13 – He divided the sea, and caused them to pass
through; and He made the waters to stand as a
heap.

Odu – The goat that breaks the drum pays for it with his
own skin.

.Lights – Green Candle w St. Peter oil

PS 79 – BABA OLOKUN:

Verse 1 - O God, the heathen are come into thine
inheritance; they holy temple have they defiled;
they have laid Jerusalem on heaps.

Verse 11 – Let the signing of the prisoner come before
thee; according to the greatness of thy power
preserve thou those that are appointed to die;

Odu – That which was agreed upon has been fulfilled.

Lights – Gray Candle w Shark oil

PS 80 – BABA OBATALA:

Verse 1– Give ear, O Shepherd of Israel, thou that
leadest Joseph like a flock; thou that dewellest

between the cherubim, shine forth,

Verse 19 – Turn us again, O Lord God of hosts, cause to shine, and we shall be saved.

Odu – To not learn from mistakes, this is the biggest mistake.

Lights – White Candle w Gardenia oil

PS 81 – BABA OGUN:

Verse 1– Sing aloud unto God our strength: make a joyful noise unto the God of Jacob.

Verse 7 – Thou calledst in trouble, and I delivered thee; I answered thee in the secret place of thunder: I proved thee at the waters of Mer'ibah.

Odu – Birds of a feather will flock together.

Lights – Green & Black Candle w All Spice oil

PS 82 – BABA ESHU ELEGBA:

Verse 1– God standeth in the congregation of the mighty; He judgeth among the God's.

Verse 6 – I have said, Ye are gods; and all of you children of the Most High.

Odu – It is false like the fog, bitter like a lemon, and the embarrassment on the House.

Lights – Red & Black Candle w Sage oil

PS 83 – IYA OSHUN/OSUN:

Verse 1– Keep not thou silence, O God: hold not thy peace. And be not still, O God.

Verse 12 – Who said, Let us take to ourselves the Houses of God in possession.

Odu – Patience is the Father of Good Character.

Lights – Yellow Candle w Crown of Success oil

PS 84 – Iya Yemoja/Yemanja:

Verse 1– How amiable are thy tabernacles, O Lord of Hosts!

Verse 10 – For a day in thy courts is better than a thousand. I had rather be a doorkeeper in the house of God, than to dwell in the tents of wickedness.

Odu – You were born to be the head and not the tail.

Lights – Blue Candle w Power oil

PS 85 – Iya Oba:

Verse 1– Lord, Thou hast been favorable unto thy land: Thou hast brought back the captivity of Jacob.

Verse 11 – Truth shall spring out of the Earth, and righteousness shall look down from Heaven.

Odu – You do not know the good that you have until you lose it.

Lights – Pink Candle w Easy Life oil

PS 86 – Iya Yemoja/Yemanja:

Verse 1– Bow down thine Ear, O Lord, hear me for I am poor and needy.

Verse 15 – But thou, O Lord, art a God full of compassion, and gracious, long-suffering, and plenteous in mercy and truth.

Odu – The tiger that eats the bone has satisfaction in his throat.

Lights – Red or White Candle w Knowledge oil

PS 87 – BABA OBATALA:

Verse 1– His foundation is in the holy mountains.

Verse 6 – The Lord shall count, when he writeth up the people, that this man was born there. Selah

Odu – One can never know all things, for Olo'dumare (God) dispersed all knowledge evenly throughout the world

Lights – White Candle w Pear oil

PS 88 – BABA OBATALA:

Verse 1– O Lord God of my salvation, I have cried day and night before thee:

Verse 12 – Shall thy wonders be known in the dark; and thy righteous in the land of forgetfulness?

Odu – Bit by bit, we eat the head of the rat.

Lights – White Candle w Vanilla oil

PS 89 – Iya Oya Yansa:

Verse 1– I will sing of the mercies of the Lord for ever: with my mouth will I make known thy faithfulness to all generations.

Verse 14 – Justice and judgment are the habitation of thy throne: mercy and truth shall before thy face.

Odu – Do good and speak truth: this is what the Orishas want.

Lights –Brown Candle w Castor oil

PS 90 – IYA OYA YANSA:

Verse 1– Lord, thou hast been our dwelling place in all generations.

Verse 16 – Let thy work appear unto thy servants and
thy glory unto their children.

Odu – Change is coming.

Lights – Brown Candle w Dark Musk oil

PS 91 – BABA OLOKUN:

Verse 1– He that dwelleth in the secret place of the Most
High shall abide under the shadow of the
Almighty.

Verse 11 – For shall give his angels charge over thee, to
keep thee in all thy ways.

Odu – Envy brings gossip.

Lights – Gray Candle w Peppermint oil

PS 92 – EGUNS:

Verse 1– It is a good thing to give thanks unto the Lord
and to sing praises unto thy name, O Most High.

Verse 13 – Those that be planted in the house of the Lord
shall floursh in the courts of our God.

Odu – There will be confusion among your friends and
family.

Lights – Multi Colored Candle w 7 African oil

PS 93 – BABA OGUN:

Verse 1– The Lord reigneth, he is clothed with majesty;
the Lord is clothed with strength, wherewith he
hath girded himself: the world also is established,
that it cannot moved.

Verse 5 – Thy testimonies are very sure; holiness
becometh thine house, O Lord, for ever.

Odu – The store house of knowledge

Lights – Green Candle w Mental Crystal oil

PS 94 – BABA SANGO/SHANGO:

Verse 1– O Lord God, to whom vengeance belongeth; O God, to whom vengeance belongeth, show thyself.

Verse 22 – But the Lord is my defenses; and my God is the rock of my refuge.

Odu – Always look to see what is before you and what is behind you.

Lights – Red Candle w Red Storax oil

PS 95 – BABA OLOKUN:

Verse 1– O come, let us sing unto the Lord: let us make a joyful noise to the rock of our salvation.

Verse 4 – In his hand are the deep places of the earth: the strength of the hills is his also.

Odu – Change and falsehood follow

Lights – Gray Candle w Tuberose Perfume oil

PS 96 – IYA OSHUN/OSUN:

Verse 1– O sing unto the Lord a new song: sing unto the Lord, all the earth.

Verse 11 – Let the heavens rejoice, and let the earth be glad; let the sea roar, and the fullness thereof.

Odu – Two rams cannot drink together at the same foundation.

Lights – Yellow Candle w Orange Kolonia 1800 Cologne

PS 97 – IYA OYA YANSA:

Verse 1– The Lord reigneth; let the earth rerjoice; let the multitude of isles be glad thereof.

Verse 9 – For thou, Lord art high above all the earth; thou art exalted far above all gods.

Odu – One born to use a hammer will see nails from heaven

Lights – Purple Candle w Violet oil

PS 98 – IYA OYA YANSA:

Verse 1– O sing unto the Lord a new song; for he hath done marvelous things; his right hand, and his holy arm, hath gotten him the victory.

Verse 5 – Sing unto the Lord with the harp; with the harp and the voice of a psalm.

Odu – Treason among friends [is certain]

Lights – Purple Candle w Violet oil

PS 99 – IYA OYA YANSA:

Verse 1– The Lord reigneth; let the people tremble: he sitteth between the cherubim; let the earth be moved.

Verse 8 – Thou answeredst them, O Lord our God; thou wast a God that forgavest them, through thou tookest vengeance of their inventions.

Odu – The greater the friend, the greater the enemy.

Lights – Brown Candle w Keep Away Enemies oil

PS 100 – BABA OBATALA:

Verse 1– Make a joyful noise unto the Lord, all ye lands.

Verse 5 – For the Lord is good; his mercy is everlasting;

and his truth endureth to all generations.

Odu – When the father leads his child follows.

Lights – White Candle w Blessed oil

PS 101 – BABA ESHU ELEGBA:

Verse 1– I will sing of mercy and judgment: unto thee, O Lord, will I sing.

Verse 16 – I will early destroy all the wicked of the land; that I may cut off all wicked doers from the city of the Lord.

Odu – The knife that slices the bread can kill a man.

Lights – Red/Black Candle w Espanta Muerto oil

PS 102 – BABA ESHU ELEGBA:

Verse 1– Hear my prayer, O Lord, and let my cry come unto thee.

Verse 27 – But thou art the same , and they shall have no end.

Odu – Carelessness will injure both you and your best friend.

Lights – White Candle w Mile and Distance oil

PS 103 – BABA ESHU ELEGBA:

Verse 1– Bless the Lord, O my soul; and all that is within me, bless his holy name.

Verse 9 – He will not always chide: neither will he keep his anger for ever.

Odu – A good roster knows when to crow.

Lights – White Candle w Elegba Cologne

PS 104 – BABA SANGO/SHANGO:

Verse 1– Bless the Lord, O my soul. O Lord my God, thou art very great; thou art clothed with honor and majesty;

Verse 7 – At thy rebuke they fled; at the voice of thy thunder they hasted away.

Odu – In the land that you travel do what you see.

Lights – Red Candle w Apple Blossom oil

PS 105 – BABA ESHU ELEGBA:

Verse 1– O give thanks unto the Lord; call upon his name; make known his deeds among the people.

Verse 45 – That they might observe his statues and keep his laws and praise Ye the Lord

Odu – If you don't know what to do for yourself, what can any one else tell you?

Lights – Red/Black Candle w Spanish H. Moss oil

PS 106 – BABA SANGO/SHANGO:

Verse 1– Praise ye the Lord, O give thanks unto the Lord; for he is good; for his mercy endureth for ever.

Verse 47 – Save us, O Lord our God and gather us from among the heathen, to give thanks unto they holy name, and to triumph in thy praise.

Odu – If you don't lose your head, you can save yourself.

Lights – Rd Candle w Redwood oil

PS 107 – IYA YEMOJA/YEMAJA:

Verse 1– O give thanks unto the Lord, for he is good; for

his mercy endureth for ever.

Verse 19 – Then they cry unto the Lord in their trouble, and he saveth them out of their distresses.

Odu – One who dreams with the dead or with the sea cannot fear either one.

Lights – Blue/White Candle w Moon oil

PS 108 – BABA OBATALA:

Verse 1– O God, my heart is fixed; I will sing and give praise, even with my glory.

Verse 13 – Through God we shall do valiantly: for he it is that shall tread down our enemies.

Odu – The war is silent and you already know it.

Lights – White Candle w Jupiter oil

PS 109 – IYA OYA YANSA:

Verse 1– Hold not thy peace, O God of my praise;

Verse 5 – And they have rewarded me evil for good, and hatred for my love.

Odu – Failures from the past will impede the future.

Lights – Brown Candle w Jinx Removing oil

PS 110 – BABA OBATALA:

Verse 1– The Lord said unto my Lord, Sit thou at my right hand, until I make thine enemies thy footstool.

Verse 7 – He shall drink of the brook in the way: therefore shall he lift up the head.

Odu – He who strives for gold gets copper instead.

Lights – White Candle w Temple oil

PS 111 – Baba Eshu Elegba:

Verse 1– Praise ye the Lord. I will praise the Lord with my whole heart, in the assembly of the upright, and in the congregation.

Verse 3 – His work is honorable and glorious: and his righteousness endureth for ever.

Odu – He who is stubborn and a pest ends up bad; his bones will rot in jail

Lights – White Candle w Court oil

PS 112 – Baba Sango/Shango:

Verse 1– Praise ye the Lord. Blessed is the man feareth the Lord, that delighteth greatly in his commandments.

Verse 7 – He shall not be afraid of evil tidings: his heart is fixed, trusting in the Lord.

Odu – Do not fight fire with a few drops of water.

Lights – Red Candle w Coffee oil

PS 113 – Baba Babalu Aiye:

Verse 1– Praise ye the Lord. Praise, O ye servants of the Lord, praise the name of the Lord.

Verse 6 – Who humbleth himself to behold the things that are in heaven, and in the earth!

Odu – That which you complain about is your own fault.

Lights – White Candle w Camphor oil

PS 114 – Baba Obatala:

Verse 1 – When Israel went out of Egypt, the house of

Jacob from a people of strange language;

Verse 8 – Which turned the rock into a standing water, the flint into a fountain of waters.

Odu – You'll sell your own luck.

Lights – White Candle w Pear oil

PS 115 – BABA SANGO/SHANGO:

Verse 1 – Not unto us, O Lord, not unto us, but unto thy name give glory, for thy mercy, and for thy truth's sake.

Verse 17 – The dead praise no the Lord, neither any that go down into silence.

Odu – Death is not far.

Lights – Red & White Candle w Cedar wood oil

PS 116 – BABA ORUNNILA:

Verse 1 – I love the Lord, because he hath heard my voice and my supplications.

Verse 13 – I will take the cup of salvation, and call upon the name of the Lord.

Odu – When the mouth ate the food, the food was defecated for being disobedient.

Lights – Green & Yellow Candle w Mastic (gum)

PS 117 – BABA ESHU ELEGBA:

Verse 1 – O praise the Lord, all ye nations: praise him, all ye people.

Verse 2 – For his merciful kindness is great toward use: and the truth of the Lord endureth for ever. Praise ye the Lord.

Odu – Eleggua saves you from death.

Lights – Red & Black Candle w Nutmeg oil

PS 118 – BABA ESHU ELEGBA:

Verse 1 – O give thanks unto the lord; for he is good:
  because his mercy endureth for ever

Verse 6 – The Lord is on my side; I will not fear: what
  can man do unto me?

Odu – He who eats too much will get sick.

Lights – Red & Black Candle w Rosemary oil

PS 119 – BABA ESHU ELEGBA:

Verse 1 – Blessed are the undefiled in the way, who walk
  in the law of the Lord.

Verse 41 – Let thy mercies come also unto me, O Lord,
  even thy salvation, according to thy word.

Odu – A flag planted will help win the war.

Lights – Red & Black Candle w Vence Edor oil

PS 120 – BABA SANGO/SHANGO:

Verse 1 – In my distress I cried unto the Lord, and he
  heard me.

Verse 7 – I am for peace: but when I speak, they are for
  war.

Odu – Those who sacrifice to the Orishas will
  accomplish their destines.

Lights – Red & White Candle w Chango Macho perfume

PS 121 – BABA ESHU ELEGBA:

Verse 1 – I will left up mine eyes unto the hills, from
  whence cometh my help.

Verse 6 – The sun shall not smite thee by day, nor the
moon by night.

Odu – The speaker dies by his own words.

Lights – Red & Black Candle w Paradise oil

PS 122– BABA SANGO/SHANGO:

Verse 1 – I was glad when they said unto me, Let us go
into the house of the Lord.

Verse 9 – Because of the house of the Lord our God I will
seek thy good.

Odu – The brothers are enemies.

Lights – White Candle w Jerusalem oil

PS 123 – BABA OGUN:

Verse 1 – Unto thee lift I up mine eyes, O thou that
dwellest in the heavens.

Verse 3 – have mercy upon us, O Lord, have mercy upon
us: for we are exceedingly filled with contempt.

Odu – One person will throw the stone and all will carry
the blame.

Lights – Green & Blue Candle w Three Kings oil

PS 124 – BABA OBATALA:

Verse 1 – If it had not been the Lord who was on our
side, now may Israel say;

Verse 8 – Our help is in the name of the Lord, who made
heaven and earth.

Odu – Chickens were born to lay eggs. You were born to
have children; do not avoid it.

Lights – White Candle w Dream oil

PS 125 – BABA SANGO/SHANGO:

Verse 1 – They that trust in the Lord shall be as mount Zion, which cannot be removed, but abideth for ever.

Verse 4 – Do good, O Lord, unto those that be good, and to them that are upright in their heart.

Odu – Everything in this life has its time.

Lights – Red Candle w 5 Finger Grass oil

PS 126 – IYA YEMOJA/YEMAJA:

Verse 1 – When the Lord turned again the captivity of Zion, we were like them that dream.

Verse 5 – They that sow in tears shall reap in joy.

Odu – From the lie shall the truth be born.

Lights – Blue Candle w Spear mint oil

PS 127 – BABA OBATALA:

Verse 1 – Except the Lord build the house, they labor in vain that build it: except the Lord keep the city, the watchman waketh but in vain.

Verse 4 – As arrows are in the hand of a mighty man; so are children of the youth.

Odu – The ear is smaller than the head, but it does not go through it.

Lights – White Candle w Efun powder

PS 128 – BABA SANGO/SHANGO:

Verse 1 – Blessed is every one that feareth the Lord; that walketh in his ways.

Verse 4 – Behold, that thus shall the man be blessed that
      feareth the Lord.

Odu – The head must carry the body and not the tail.

Lights – Red Candle w Sun oil

PS 129 – BABA AGANYU:

Verse 1 – Many a time have they afflicted me from my
      youth, may Israel now say:

Verse 6 – Let them be as the grass upon the house-tops,
      which withereth afore it groweth up:

Odu – One fails when one makes trouble.

Lights – Brown Candle w Oriental oil

PS 130 – BABA ORUNMILA:

Verse 1 – Out of the depths have I cried unto thee, O
      Lord.

Verse 8 – And he shall redeem Israel from all his
      iniquities.

Odu – The stone will not dig.

Lights – Green & Yellow Candle w King Solomon oil

PS 131 – IYA OSHUN/OSUN:

Verse 1 – Lord, my heart is not haughty, nor mine eyes
      lofty: neither do I exercise myself in great matters,
      or in things too high for me.

Verse 3 – Let Israel hope in the Lord from henceforth
      and for ever.

Odu – Oche' is the blood that runs through the veins.

Lights – Yellow Candle w Sunflower oil

PS 132 – Baba Sango/Shango:

Verse 1 – Lord, remember David, and all his afflictions:

Verse 7 – We will go into his tabernacles: we will worship at his footstool.

Odu – As intelligent as quail are, they still sleep on the ground.

Lights – Red Candle w Saffron powder

PS 133 – Iya Yemoja/Yemaja:

Verse 1 – Behold, how good and how pleasant it is for brethren to dwell together in unity.

Verse 3 – As the dew of Hermon, and as the dew that descended upon the mountains of Zion: for there the Lord commanded the blessing, even life for evermore.

Odu – In Odi, the hole (the grave) is finally dug.

Lights – Blue & White Candle w House Blessing oil

PS 134 – Baba Obatala:

Verse 1 – Behold, bless ye the Lord, all ye servants of the Lord, which by night stand in the house of the Lord.

Verse 3 – The Lord that made heaven and earth bless thee out of Zion.

Odu – Remember: It is the head that carries the body; do not lose the head.

Lights – White Candle w Oar Moss oil

PS 135 – Baba Aganyu:

Verse 1 – Praise ye the Lord. Praise ye the name of the Lord; praise him, O ye servants of the Lord.

Verse 16 – They have mouths, but they speak not; eyes have they, but they see not;

Odu – Your friend is great; the evil that he brings will be great as well.

Lights – Brown Candle w St. Chrisphor oil

PS 136 – BABA OBATALA:

Verse 1 – O give thanks unto the Lord; for he is good: for his mercy endureth for ever.

Verse 26 – O give thanks unto the God of heaven for his mercy endureth for ever.

Odu – Even deep in the forest, a fire cannot hide.

Lights – White Candle w Our Lady of Mercies oil

PS 137 – EGUN:

Verse 1 – By the rivers of Babylon, there we sat down, yea, we wept, when we remembered Zion.

Verse 4 – How shall we sing the Lord's song in a strange land?

Odu – When there is more on the ground than in the basket, one wasted his blessing.

Lights – Multi-Colored Candle w Olive oil

PS 138 – BABA OBATALA:

Verse 1 – I will praise thee with my whole heart: before the gods will I sing praise unto thee.

Verse 5 – Yea, they shall sing in the ways of the Lord: for great is the glory of the Lord.

Odu – A wise man will never try to be king; he will be the advisor to the king and no more.

Lights – White Candle w All Saints oil

PS 139 – Baba Orunmila:

Verse 1 – O Lord, thou hast searched me, and known me.

Verse 20 – For they speak against thee wickedly, and thine enemies take thy name in vain.

Odu – Take the water from the river, you destroy the home of fish.

Lights – Green & Yellow Candle w Van Van oil

PS 140 – Baba Eshu Elegba:

Verse 1 – Deliver me, O Lord, from the evil man: preserve me from the violent man;

Verse 13 – Surely the righteous shall give thanks unto thy name: the upright shall dwell in thy presence.

Odu – There is fire within and fire without.

Lights – Red & Black Candle w Arabian Bouquet oil

PS 141 – Baba Sango/Shango:

Verse 1 – Lord, I cry unto thee: make haste unto me; give ear unto my voice, when I cry unto thee.

Verse 10 – Let the wicked fall into their own nets, whilst that I withal escape.

Odu – When Oro sounds, men become silent.

Lights – Red Candle w Tonka Bean oil

PS 142 – Iya Yemoja/Yemaja:

Verse 1 – I cried unto the Lord with my voice; with my voice unto the Lord did I make my supplication.

Verse 7 – Bring my soul out of prison, that I praise they
name: the righteous shall compass me about; for
thou shall bountifully with me.

Odu – In adultery, there will always be danger.

Lights – Blue Candle w Trinity oil

PS 143 – BABA OBATALA:

Verse 1 – Hear my prayer, O Lord, give ear to my
supplications: in thy faithfulness answer me, and
in thy righteousness.

Verse 6 – I stretch forth my hands unto thee: my soul
thirsteh after thee, as a thirsty land. Selah.

Odu – Only one King can govern a town.

Lights – White Candle w Holiness powder & Olive oil

PS 144 – IYA OYA YANSA:

Verse 1 – Blessed be the Lord my strength, which
teacheth my hands to war, and my fingers to fight.

Verse 4 – Happy is that people, that is in such a case:
yea, happy is that people, whose God is the Lord.

Odu – That which has been left behind should be left
behind.

Lights – Brown Candle w Nine Mystery oil

PS 145 – BABA OBATALA:

Verse 1 – I will extol thee, my God, O King; and I will
bless thy name for ever and ever.

Verse 9 – The Lord is good to all: and his tender mercies
are over all his works.

Odu – Beside the river, the silk cotton tree cannot hide.

Lights – White Candle w Obeah oil

PS 146 – BABA BABALUAIYE:

Verse 1 – Praise ye the Lord, Praise the Lord, O my soul.

Verse 3 – Put not your trust in princes, nor in the son of man, in whom there is no help.

Odu – When money is scarce, the search for work begins: when one feels thirst, one travels to the well, when hunger pangs are felt, one seeks out food: only when a need becomes known does one begin his search, for need is beginning of fulfillment.

Lights – Brown Candle w Sesame oil & seeds

PS 147 – BABA SANGO/SHANGO:

Verse 1 – Praise ye Lord: for its is good to sing praises unto our God; for it is pleasant; and praise is comely.

Verse 15 – He sendeth forth his commandment upon earth: his word runneth very swiftly.

Odu – A knife no matter how long or how sharp can never carry its own handle.

Lights – Red Candle w (Red) Pepper oil

PS 148 – BABA BABALU AIYE:

Verse 1 – Praise ye the Lord. Praise ye the Lord from the heavens: praise him in the heights

Verse 7 – Praise the Lord from the earth, ye dragons, and all deeps:

Odu – It pays to stoop to conquer.

Lights – Purple Candle w High Conqueror oil

PS 149 – BABA ESHU ELEGBA:

Verse 1 – Praise ye the Lord. Sing unto the Lord a new song, and his praise in the congregation of saints.

Verse 5 – Let the saints be joyful in glory: let them sing aloud upon their beds.

Odu – Things come suddenly; you will miss your opportunities.

Lights – Red Candle w Horn of Plenty oil

PS 150 – BABA SANGO/SHANGO:

Verse 1 – Praise ye the Lord. Peace God in his sanctuary: praise him in the firmament of his power.

Verse 6 – Let every thing that hath breath praise the Lord. Praise ye the Lord.

Odu – The king does not die.

Lights – Red Candle w Maget oil

NOTES

1. THE DILOGGUN, The Orisha, Proverbs, Sacrifices, and Prohibitions of Cuban Santeria, Ocha'ni Lele, Destiny Books, Rochester, VT 2003

2. The Book Of Psalms, King James Version 1611; American Bible Society, NY 1978

INDEX

Baba Sango

Courage/Strengthen/Wisdom PS 9 PS 15 PS 31 PS 39 PS 60 PS 6

PS 76 PS 106 PS 128 PS 147

Luck/Money PS 4 PS 42 PS 66 PS 120 PS 141 PS 150

Love PS 67 PS 104 PS 132.

Enemies/Justice/Protection PS 12 PS 40 PS 94 PS 112 PS 115

Iya Oshun

Love PS 32. PS 41 PS 50 PS 58 PS 96 PS 131

Luck/Money PS 19 PS 23 PS 9 PS 54 PS 55 PS 56

Enemies/Protection PS 5 PS 14 PS 53 PS 83

Baba Olokun

Wisdom/Health PS 74

Enemies/Justice/Court Case PS 79 PS 91 PS 95

Bbaba Babalu-aiye

Luck/Money PS 11

Enemies PS 17 PS 148

Health PS 113 PS 146

Spiritual Protection PS 38

Baba Aganju

Luck PS 18

Wisdom PS 129

Health PS 135

Ibeji

All Purpose PS 20

Baba Obatala
Spiritual Wisdom/Peace/Strength PS 2 PS 8 PS 24 PS 26
PS 35
PS 44 PS 49 PS 62 PS 64 PS 68 PS 80 PS 87 PS 88 PS 100
PS
114 PS 124 PS 136 PS 138 PS 143
Enemies PS 28 PS 51 PS 145
Justice PS 110 PS 127 PS 134
Luck/Money PS 72 PS 108

Iya Oba
Love/Marriage PS 85

Baba Osanyin
With the Warriors

Baba Erinle
With Iya Yemoja

Eguns [ancestors]
Spiritual Protection PS 69
Health PS 137
Money/Luck/Job/Court Case PS 92

Nana Buruko
All Purpose/Works with Babalu Aiye PS 13

Orisha Oko
Work with the Warriors PS 29

Baba Orunmila
Wisdom/Spiritual/Protection/Guidance PS 16 PS 65 PS
116 PS 130
Enemies/Justice PS 57
Luck/Money/Job PS 139

Iya Yemoja

Spiritual Protection/Wisdom/Cleanings of: Mind,
Spirit/Strengthen
PS 7 PS 52 PS 70 PS 77 PS 84 PS 86 PS 107 PS 142
Love PS 47
Luck/Money PS 71
Enemies PS 126

Bio:

Iya Akousa Claudette Culver, has many paths and roads in her spiritual growth and journey. She is devotee of God and worships on many levels. Her spiritual life changed forever in the 1980's. Became a High Priestess in Wicca -1983; Initiated into the Mayan Order - 1984; Crown Obatala in Ocha - 1988; Ordain Bishop in Metaphysics - 1996; Initiated for Maha Kali - 2005. Iya governs Ile *Shango Dina* in Brooklyn, NY since 1989 till present.